Making Sense Out of Life

WHAT'S YOUR POINT?

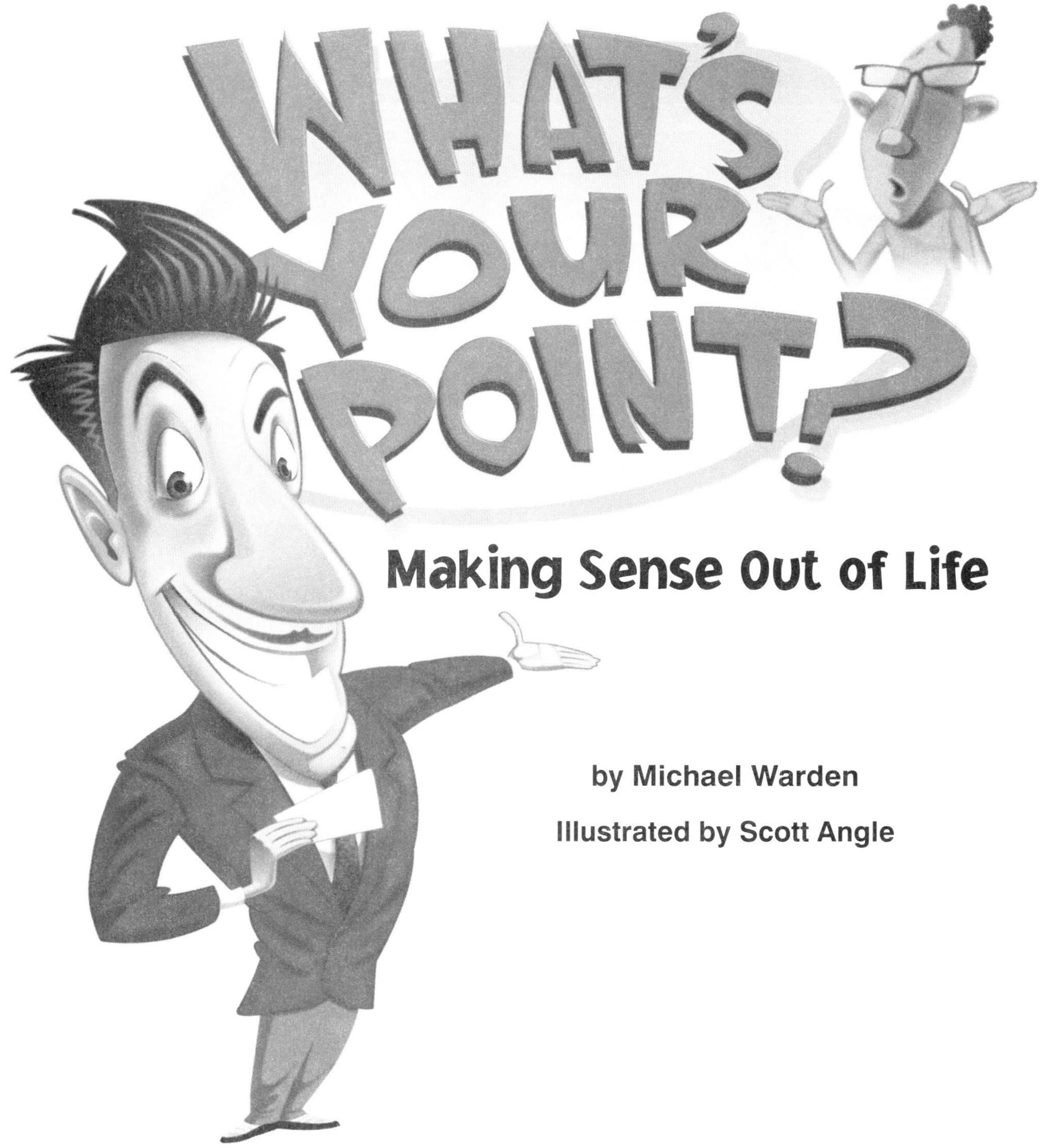

Making Sense Out of Life

by Michael Warden

Illustrated by Scott Angle

A creative study of the book of Colossians

Standard Publishing
Cincinnati, Ohio

Table of Contents

Cover illustration by Scott Angle
Inside design by Dina Sorn
Edited by Dale Reeves and Leslie Durden

© 1999 by Standard Publishing.
All rights reserved.
Printed in the United States of America.

The Standard Publishing Company,
Cincinnati, Ohio.
A division of Standex International Corporation.

06   05   04   03   02   01   00   99

5   4   3   2   1

ISBN: 0-7847-0952-1

How to Use This Book

I once heard a true story about a missionary who got lost in the African jungle while trying to reach a remote village. After wandering around in the bush for some time, he caught sight of a hut, and quickly went to ask the family if there was anyone who could lead him out of the jungle to his destination. The father of the family, who was native to the area, agreed to help.

"Thank you," said the missionary. "Please show me the way."

"Walk," said the native, and abruptly started off into the bush. For more than an hour, the missionary followed the man, hacking his way through the thick growth of unmarked jungle. Eventually the missionary began to worry that the native didn't really know where he was going.

"Are you sure this is the way?" asked the missionary.

"Yes," said the native.

"But where is the path?" he asked.

The native stopped and said, "Bwana, in this place there is no path. I am the path."

In John 14:6, Jesus said, "'I am the way and the truth and the life. No one comes to the Father except through me.'" At times in our lives as Christians, we may find it hard to focus on Jesus as the "path" we must follow. Too often, we want rules and traditions to direct us instead. That's because following a rule is easier than depending on Jesus in a personal way. We know he is the point of life. However, we are easily enticed by traditions and religious regulations that may sound good, but invariably distract us from the truth.

In this world, there is no path. Jesus is the path.[1]

That's why the Apostle Paul wrote the book of Colossians. The Christians at Colosse had committed themselves to following Jesus as the "path" and acknowledging him as the "point" of their lives. But something was beginning to go wrong. Outside influences had come into the church—false Christians who were telling the Colossians that the point of life wasn't following Jesus; rather, it was to adhere to their strict religious traditions of self-denial in order to achieve a higher spiritual enlightenment. These false teachers managed to distract many of the Colossians from focusing on the true point of life—following Jesus—and got them to focus instead on things that didn't really matter.

In response, Paul directed the Colossians to turn their attention back to Jesus—and to recognize his lordship over their lives. Paul strongly emphasized the preeminence of Christ over everything in creation, calling him:

• the Creator and Sustainer of all things (1:16, 17)

- the head over every power and authority (2:10)
- the full embodiment of Deity (1:15; 2:9)
- the Redeemer and Reconciler (1:14, 20-22)
- the resurrected Lord (1:18; 3:1)
- the all-sufficient Savior (1:28; 2:3; 3:1-4)
- the Head of the church (1:18)
- the basis for the believer's hope (1:5, 23, 27)
- the source of the believer's power for a new life (1:11, 29)

But Paul didn't just address Christ's lordship. He also gave specific instructions for how that lordship should impact our lives. If Christ is the point of our lives, what, then, should our lives look like? That's the question Paul answers for the Colossians, and his answers still hold true for Christians today.

This book is designed to help you guide your students to explore the truths and challenges contained in Paul's letter to the Colossians—and discover for themselves how focusing on following Jesus as the point of their lives will not only transform their hearts but also powerfully impact the world around them.

Each session in this book is divided into three sections: **State Your Case, Cut to the Chase** and **Make Your Point.** Each of these sections contains more than one option or activity for you to use, depending on your needs and the needs of your students.

In the **State Your Case** section, you'll find two creative ideas for introducing the study to your group. Typically, one idea is more active than the other. Choose whichever option you think would work best with your students.

In the **Cut to the Chase** section, you'll find three Bible activities that will help students creatively explore specific sections of the book of Colossians. The first two activities in this section are designed to work together as an experiential study of the Scripture, combined with interactive small-group debriefing and application. The third activity is typically less active and uses real-life quotes, stories or other activities to encourage discussion about the Scripture and its application to daily life. You may choose to do only the first two activities, or just the third or all three, depending on your time limitations and the needs of your group.

In the **Make Your Point** section, you'll find two closing options to help students take what they've learned and immediately apply it to their lives. The first option uses a variety of approaches to help solidify the learning in their lives and challenge them to apply what they've learned. The second option offers students a more specific challenge each week for applying what they've learned to their lives in a practical way. Feel free to select the closing that's most appropriate for your group.

Each session also features **Check This** suggestions for using contemporary Christian music that reinforces the point you are trying to make. Each song is meant to be woven into your presentation of the material. Without proper explanation before or after, it will become merely entertainment and not a teaching tool.

At the conclusion of each study, be sure to distribute copies of the reproducible midweek devotional guide, **Get to the Point!,** to encourage your teenagers to dig into God's Word during the week.

When God Dreams 1

In this session, your students will use a variety of creative methods to examine and illustrate God's dream or purpose for creating them, as recorded in Colossians 1:1-14. Then they'll evaluate their own personal dreams in light of what they discover about God's purpose for their lives. Through this examination, they can learn why it's so important to make every day count by pursuing God's purpose for their lives.

State Your Case

1 AN IDEAL WORLD

Before your teens arrive, cut a supersize "globe" shape from a large sheet of newsprint. Lay the globe shape out on the floor, then set out colored markers. Once students arrive, form five groups and assign each group one of these categories: Science, Art, Social Issues, Religion or Family.

Begin this activity by saying, **"We're going to start today's session by creating a mural that illustrates what life would be like in a world where all our dreams for humanity actually came true."**

Divide the newsprint globe into five sections and assign each group a different section. Then say, **"In your groups, discuss what life would be like in an ideal world within your assigned category. For example, in an ideal world, what would be the role of science? What kinds of accomplishments would science have achieved in an ideal world? Or in the family category, you could ask yourselves what families would be like in an ideal world. How would family members relate to one another?"**

Have groups discuss their dreams for humanity, then work together to create a section of the mural to represent or illustrate those dreams. For example, in the family category, group members might draw a family enjoying life together or fill the space with symbols such as hearts or peace signs. Allow groups about five minutes to create their mural sections.

When groups are finished, have each group take turns explaining its mural. Then discuss these questions:

• **How does it feel to think about our dreams in this way?**

LESSON TEXT
Colossians 1:1-14

LESSON FOCUS
God has a dream for your life.

LESSON GOALS
As a result of participating in this lesson, students will:
• Explore God's hopes and dreams for humanity.
• Discover specific reasons why God created them.
• Examine their personal dreams in light of God's purpose for their lives.

Materials needed:
Newsprint; scissors; colored markers

The overriding theme of Colossians is the supremacy of Christ in and over all things. Paul most likely focused on this theme because of heresies that were threatening the faith and behavior of the Christians at Colosse. They were in danger of losing sight of the point of their lives—knowing, loving and serving Jesus Christ. In response, Paul didn't try to dismantle wrong beliefs. Instead, he drew the readers' focus back to the preeminence of Jesus.

In the same way, your students are threatened by all kinds of false beliefs about the nature and purpose of life. Rather than try to refute all those lies, we can best help teens by drawing their focus to Christ, helping them understand who he is and what his place should be in life. He is the point of life. When teenagers really see this, other lesser points will tend to lose their appeal.

Check This . . .
A great song to help introduce this session is "Lord of the Dance," recorded by Steven Curtis Chapman on his album *Signs of Life*. The song "Land of Opportunity," from the same album, also fits well with this study.

Materials needed:
Bibles; newsprint; markers; paper; writing utensils

- Based on what we created, do you think we all have a lot of similar dreams for humanity? Why or why not?
- Do you think our dreams will ever come true? Why or why not?

Conclude the discussion by saying, **"God gave us all the ability to dream, perhaps so that we could imagine what's possible, rather than only be able to see what 'is.' In fact, the capacity to dream is one of the ways we are created in God's image. God also has dreams for humanity—and for each one of us as individuals. When he looks at us, he sees not only what 'is'; he also sees what could be. Today we're beginning a new study of the book of Colossians. In the coming weeks, we'll learn about the dreams God had in mind when he created us, and we'll discover how pursuing God's dreams for us can give great purpose and meaning to our lives. Let's begin by taking a look at God's dream for us."**

2 DREAM ANALYSIS

Have your students form pairs. Each one should tell the other about a dream he or she has had (while sleeping) that left a strong impression. For example, did they ever dream that someone close to them was in trouble and later call to make sure that person was OK? Or have they ever dreamed they were flying and now want to learn to fly an airplane?

When pairs finish, ask for a few volunteers to share about their partner's dream. Then ask:

- **Why do you think we dream?**
- **Why do dreams like the ones we've discussed impact us so much?**
- **Do you think God dreams in the same way we do? Why or why not?**
- **Do you think God has "dreams" about each of us? Why or why not?**
- **If God dreamed about you, what do you hope he would dream?**

Conclude by saying, **"God may not have sleeping dreams in the way we do, but he *does* have dreams for each of us. It was probably those dreams that prompted him to create us in the first place. But what are his dreams for us? What is the reason he created us? Today we're beginning a new study of Colossians. In that book we can actually get a glimpse of God's dreams for each of us and humanity as a whole. Through this study, we're going to discover not only what God's dreams are for you, but also how pursuing those dreams can bring a great sense of purpose and meaning to life. Let's begin by taking a look at God's dream for us."**

Cut to the Chase

1 CREATIVE DREAMSCAPES

Form five groups. (If you did option 1 in the opening activity, you can just have teens stay in their groups.) Have groups read Colossians 1:1-14, then discuss this question: **"How is this passage a reflection of God's dream for humanity? for you personally?"**

Say, **"Different people express their dreams in different ways. In this passage, Paul is expressing God's dream for us in the form of a prayer. Let's take a little challenge and see if we can come up with some other creative ways to express God's dream based on these verses."**

Assign each group one of the following creative challenges based on God's dream recorded in Colossians 1:1-14:

- Draw a picture that illustrates God's dream.
- Write a speech that God might give to explain his dream. Start the speech with the words, "I have a dream . . ."
- Write a song that expresses God's dream.
- Act out a story that demonstrates God's dream in action.
- Find a series of objects in the church or outside that could represent different aspects of God's dream.

After each group has its assignment, make sure students understand what they're supposed to do. Then allow groups 10 minutes to complete their projects.

When groups are finished, have each group present its project to the whole group. After all the presentations, discuss these questions:

- **What did you like most about these various presentations?**
- **Does the passage in Colossians hold more meaning to you now that we've done these projects? Why or why not?**
- **How did applying our creativity help bring the message of God's dream to life in our minds?**
- **Do you want God's dream to come true in your life? Why or why not?**

Conclude this activity by saying, "**We've seen a glimpse of our own creative powers in this activity. But God has creative power that far exceeds anything we can do. And God wants to work creatively in our lives to make his dreams for us come true. But before that can happen, we have to understand what his dreams are and then choose them for ourselves as well. Let's take a closer look at the dream God has for humanity.**"

2 GOD'S GLOBAL DREAM

If you did option 1 in the opening activity, pull out the newsprint globe and turn it over so that the blank faces up. If you didn't do option 1, cut out a supersize "globe" shape from a large piece of newsprint. Set out colored markers. Tell pairs to read through the passage again and write on their papers any words or phrases that sum up or explain any aspect of God's dream for humanity. For example, based on Colossians 1:10, 11, students might write, "please God in every way," "grow in the knowledge of God" or "have great endurance, patience and joy in life." When pairs finish, have them use markers to transfer their words and phrases to the newsprint globe.

When the globe is complete, gather students around it to discuss these questions:

- **How is that globe a picture of God's dream for humanity?**
- **What surprises you about the words you see here?**
- **Would you like to live in a world where all these things were true? Why or why not?**
- **How does this picture of God's dream for the world compare to your own dreams for how you'd like the world to be?**
- **What if this globe represented God's dream for your life? Would you want to live a life in which all these things were true? Why or why not?**
- **Why do you think God wants these things for your life?**
- **Based on this word picture of God's dream for humanity, what do you think the point of life is?**
- **Does this picture accurately represent the point of your life? Why or why not?**

Materials needed:
Bibles; newsprint; scissors; paper; writing utensils; colored markers

In Colossians 1:12, Paul says that all Christians have been "qualified" to share in the inheritance of the saints. But what is this inheritance that's available to your students? Although we probably won't grasp the big picture of what that inheritance entails until we're in Heaven, the Bible does give us several clues about what God's inheritance includes. Here's a sampling: Christians inherit . . .

- the kingdom of God (Matthew 25:34; 1 Corinthians 6:9, 10)
- the earth (Matthew 5:5)
- salvation (Hebrews 1:14)
- a blessing (1 Peter 3:9)
- glory (Romans 8:17, 18)
- incorruption (1 Corinthians 15:50)
- eternal life (Luke 10:25-28)

Materials needed:
Bibles; writing utensils; reproducible student sheet on page 14 of this book

Materials needed:
Bibles; writing utensils; reproducible student sheet on page 15 of this book

Conclude the discussion by saying, "**God had a specific purpose in mind when he created each of you. He wants your life to have a point. But he leaves it up to you to decide whether you'll follow his plan for your life or try to come up with some point of your own. No matter what you try, though, you can't out-dream God. His dream for you will always be bigger and better than your dreams for yourself. That's why it makes so much sense to let God give purpose to your life. He has a dream . . . and you're it.**"

3 DISCOVERING YOUR POINT IN LIFE

Form groups of six or fewer, perhaps based on their favorite "philosopher"—Dear Abby, Dr. Laura, Dilbert, Calvin & Hobbes or Dave Barry. Give each person a copy of the reproducible student sheet on page 14 and a writing utensil. Say, "**On this sheet you'll find several quotes from various people about the meaning or point of life. Read the quotes in your group, then discuss the questions listed after them.**"

After the discussion, say, "**The Bible says that 'we all, like sheep, have gone astray, each of us has turned to his own way' (Isaiah 53:6). There are lots of ideas out there about the true meaning and purpose of life. But we can find the real point of life just by asking the One who created life in the first place. He has a purpose for me, for you and for everyone you know. He alone knows the point of our existence. And if we follow him, we will each discover it for ourselves.**"

Make Your Point

1 MY POINT EXACTLY

Give each person a writing utensil and a copy of the "My Point Exactly" reproducible student sheet on page 15. Instruct students to write in the globe shape a personal "dream for my life" based on God's dream for humanity recorded in Colossians 1:1-14. When they finish, have them write their names on the back of the handout and then tape it (name side up) to one of the walls.

Say, "**What you wrote is between you and God. No one will look at these during this study. When we've completed our study of Colossians, we will look at them again and see if anything about our dreams have changed.**"

Close with prayer, asking God to reveal his point in creating each person present.

REFLECTING ON THE LESSON

Form pairs, and have partners take turns telling each other the way they would complete these sentences:

- **One important thing I've learned from this lesson is . . . .**
- **One thing I'll do this week to help me apply what I've learned today is . . . .**

If you have time, encourage students to tell the whole group how they completed the previous sentences. Distribute copies of **Get to the Point!**, the mid-week devotional found on page 16, to each student. Conclude by saying, **"This week, choose to be extraordinary by taking the challenge written on your handout. Then tell us all about it next week."**

Close with prayer.

Materials needed:
Reproducible student sheet on page 16 of this book

Discovering Your Point in Life

Read these quotes in your group, then discuss the questions that follow:

"To find happiness we must seek for it in a focus outside ourselves."—W. Beran Wolfe

"The answers to Life's questions lie inside you. All you need to do is look, listen and trust."
—Cherie Carter-Scott

"To know even one other life has breathed easier because you have lived—This is to have succeeded."
—Ralph Waldo Emerson

"For life is a mystery to be lived out rather than a problem to be solved."—Anonymous

"We hold these truths to be self-evident, that all men are created equal, that they are endowed by their Creator with certain unalienable rights, that among these are life, liberty and the pursuit of happiness."
—The American Declaration of Independence

"That is happiness; to be dissolved into something complete and great."—Willa S. Cather

"Believe me! The secret of reaping the greatest fruitfulness and the greatest enjoyment from life is to live dangerously!"
—Friedrich Nietzsche

Discuss these questions:

- **What's your reaction to these quotes?**

- **How does the message in each of these quotes compare with the message of God's dream for our lives in Colossians 1:1-14?**

- **Which quote do you think comes closest to expressing God's dream for us?**

- **Which quote seems to go against God's dream for us?**

- **Why do you think people have so many different ideas about the real point of life?**

- **Based on all we've studied today, what do you think the real point of life is?**

My Point Exactly

God dreams big dreams about us. And he wants us to dream too! In the globe below, write a personal dream for your life based on Colossians 1:1-14. What you write is just between you and God.

GET TO THE POINT!

What Do You Think?

Take this handout with you as you go about your weekly routine. At least three times this week, show these quotes to someone you know, then ask them these questions:
• What's your reaction to these quotes?
• What do you think is the point of life?

"To find happiness we must seek for it in a focus outside ourselves."—W. Beran Wolfe

"The answers to Life's questions lie inside you. All you need to do is look, listen and trust."—Cherie Carter-Scott

"To know even one other life has breathed easier because you have lived—This is to have succeeded."—Ralph Waldo Emerson

"For life is a mystery to be lived out rather than a problem to be solved."—Anonymous

"We hold these truths to be self-evident, that all men are created equal, that they are endowed by their Creator with certain unalienable rights, that among these are life, liberty and the pursuit of happiness."—The American Declaration of Independence

"That is happiness; to be dissolved into something complete and great."—Willa S. Cather

"Believe me! The secret of reaping the greatest fruitfulness and the greatest enjoyment from life is to live dangerously!"—Friedrich Nietzsche

Write each person's response below, along with your own reaction to what each person said. Then tell each person what you think the point of life is all about.

1. _____
_____
_____
_____

2. _____
_____
_____

3. _____
_____
_____

Jesus Christ: The Point of Everything
2

In their culture, many things vie for center stage in the hearts of your students. Distractions abound everywhere, keeping them from serving Jesus wholeheartedly. In this session, your group will work in teams to design and create a throne suitable for Jesus to sit in. Then they'll examine Colossians 1:15–2:10 to discover how they can create a throne worthy of Jesus within their own hearts. Through this exploration, they can understand the preeminence of Christ in all creation, and learn why they need to make Jesus the preeminent point of their lives.

State Your Case

1 BEST BALLOON BATTLE

Once everyone has arrived, give each person a handful of balloons and have all the students blow them up and tie them off. Then lead them through a series of quick contests using the balloons. Keep the pace fast and encourage them to do their best. Here are some sample contests you could use:

- **Best smiley face on a balloon**—Toss each student a marker and set a time limit of 10 seconds to create the best smiling face on a balloon. When time is up, have students vote on which balloon is the best.
- **Best balloon holder**—Have students take turns trying to hold as many balloons as they can at one time for five seconds (without help from anyone else). Pronounce the person who holds the most balloons the "Best Balloon Holder on the Planet."
- **Best balloon tossers**—Quickly form groups of four and have them compete to see which team can keep the greatest number of balloons in the air continuously for five seconds. Introduce the winning team as the "Best Balloon Tossers in the Universe."
- **Best balloon buster**—Call for a race to pop all the balloons by sitting on them. Designate the person who pops the most balloons as the "Best Balloon Buster in all Creation."

After the games, gather everyone together and ask:
- **Were these games fun to you? Why or why not?**
- **How did it feel for me to name the winners as the best in that event?**

LESSON TEXT
Colossians 1:15–2:10

LESSON FOCUS
Jesus is the ultimate point of all creation.

LESSON GOALS
As a result of participating in this lesson, students will:
- Try to create a throne worthy of Jesus to sit in.
- Discover why they need to put Jesus on the throne of their lives.
- Be challenged to put Jesus on the throne of their lives.

Materials needed:
Balloons; markers

Check This . . .
If your students took the "Get to the Point!" Challenge last week, take a few minutes at the start of the session to have them share their experience with the group.

Materials needed:
Newsprint; tape; markers

Materials needed:
Bibles; a chair; colored markers; colored ribbon; colored crepe paper or cloth; cardboard; a white sheet; tape; other assorted craft items

- Do you think that title was deserved? Why or why not?
- What does it really mean to be the best?
- Do you think any one person could ever claim to be the best over everyone else? over everything in creation? Why or why not?

Read aloud Colossians 1:15-18. Then ask:

- Do you think Jesus deserves the title of the best above everything? Why or why not?

Conclude the discussion by saying, **"According to these verses, Jesus is supreme over everything in creation. That means that he represents God's ultimate best—better than the greatest athletes, more powerful than the strongest armies, wiser than the smartest people and more beautiful than the greatest beauty you can think of.**

"That's hard for us to imagine, but today we're going to take a closer look at the awesomeness of Jesus and learn why God has exalted him as the ultimate point of life for everything in creation."

ONLY THE BEST WILL DO

Before your students arrive, tape several sheets of newsprint to the walls. At the top of each sheet, write a different one of these headings: Best Food, Best Movie, Best Natural Wonder, Best President, Best Athlete, Best Singer, Best Movie Star and Best Book.

As students arrive, give them each a marker and ask them to write their choices for each category under the appropriate heading. Once everyone has voted, go through the list as a group and ask volunteers to tell why they answered the way they did. Then discuss these questions:

- **How do you determine whether someone or something is the best?**
- **Is it possible for everyone in the world to agree that a particular person is the absolute best above all others? Why or why not?**
- **Would you say Jesus is the best or most supreme over everyone and everything else? Why or why not?**

Have a volunteer read aloud Colossians 1:15-18. Then ask:

- **What do these verses say about Jesus' rank in creation?**
- **Is it hard for you to see Jesus as the supreme being over everyone and everything that exists? Why or why not?**

Say, **"Jesus outranks everything in creation as God's best. Today we're going to explore how Christ's supremacy should impact our daily choices and our purpose in life."**

Cut to the Chase

THE SEAT OF SUPREMACY

Place an empty chair at one end of the room and ask your group to sit in a semicircle around the chair. In front of the chair, spread out the supplies listed in the margin. They will be picking up some of these items to represent various characteristics of Christ. Have students open their Bibles to Colossians 1:15-20. Then say, **"We're going to read through this passage together. As we do, I'll stop and explain what some of the important words mean and what they say about Jesus. Then we'll work together to choose some items from the** supplies I've laid out to represent each of the ideas we discuss."

Have volunteers take turns reading successive verses from Colossians 1:15-20. As they read, pause to explain the following terms and ideas as they come up. (It may work best if your group reads from the *NIV* version for this activity.)

- **". . . image of the invisible God"**—The word "image" (*eikon*) denotes that Jesus didn't just "look like" God, but that he was actually a manifestation of God. Jesus supported this idea when he said, "'Anyone who has seen me has seen the Father'" (John 14:9).

Ask students to choose an item to represent God's image.

- **". . . firstborn over all creation"**—This doesn't mean that Jesus was born before everything else (in fact, since Jesus is eternal, he was never "born" in that sense at all). Rather, it's a way of describing Jesus' priority and preeminence over all creation.

Ask them to choose an item to represent Jesus' preeminence over all creation.

- **". . . thrones or powers or rulers or authorities"**—This list refers to both angelic and earthly authorities.

Ask them to choose one or more items to represent angelic and earthly authorities.

- **". . . in him all things hold together"**—This means that Jesus is more than just the big chief who runs the universe; it means he is the actual glue that holds everything together.

Ask them to choose an item to represent Christ's power to hold the universe together.

- **". . . so that in everything he might have the supremacy"**—That is, so that he might be designated as the best over everything.

Ask them to choose an item to represent Jesus' rank above everything in creation.

- **". . . God was pleased to have all his fullness dwell in him"**—This means that all of God was (and is) in Jesus. Jesus is God.

Ask them to choose an item to represent Jesus' divine nature.

Once you've read through the passage, explained the terms and had students choose items to represent those terms, form six groups and assign each group one of the six items the group chose to represent a quality of Christ. Then say, **"Work with the other groups to transform this chair into a throne that you would welcome Jesus to sit in."**

Allow the groups eight to ten minutes to complete the transformation. When they are finished, have each group explain again what its assigned item represents. Then instruct the students to discuss these questions in their groups:

- **What's your reaction to our throne?**
- **If we had unlimited money and time, how would you improve this throne?**
- **If Jesus really were going to come and join us in this meeting, what else might you do to prepare for his arrival?**
- **Why is it important that we treat Jesus with this kind of honor?**
- **How is the way we prepared this throne similar to the way God wants us to prepare our hearts for him to come and be Lord of our lives?**

Conclude the discussion by saying, **"Jesus is Lord over the universe. But he doesn't want to rule over us with an iron fist. He wants our relationship with him to be based on love. That's why he doesn't force us to follow him. He leaves it up to us to come to him and ask him to come into our lives and lead us. Let's take a closer look at what it means for us to do that."**

2 MY THRONE

Have students form a circle. Give each person a writing utensil and a copy of the "My Throne" student sheet on page 22 of this book. Say, **"In the box at the bottom of the handout, list all the things, people and activities that are the most important to you: your friends, your school, your appearance, your future, your sports, your hobbies, your parents and family—anything that really matters to you. Then, on the throne draw pictures or write words that represent the top five important things in your life. Put the most important thing at the top of the throne, then place the rest in order somewhere beneath. When we're finished, we'll share what we created."**

Allow students about five minutes to complete their creations. When time is up, have them find a partner and explain the throne creation to him or her. Then have pairs discuss these questions:

- **How does your personal life throne compare with the throne we created earlier?**
- **If someone you didn't know examined your life, what do you think he or she would say is your purpose in life?**
- **What do you want your life to say to other people?**
- **What do you want your life to say about Jesus?**
- **Is Jesus "Lord" of all of your life? Why or why not?**
- **How would your life change if living for Jesus was your main goal in life?**

After the discussion, have volunteers share what they discussed in their pairs. Then conclude, **"God has already made Jesus the ultimate point of all creation. One day everyone and everything will bow to his authority and recognize his rightful place as ruler over everything. But for now, Jesus will not force us to serve him. He wants us to come willingly, because we love him and respect his authority over our lives. He is the point of life—but you have to choose him."**

3 JESUS WHO?

Form three groups, possibly by having students choose their favorite ice cream from among chocolate, strawberry and vanilla. If they haven't already read through Colossians 1:15–2:10, have them do that in their groups. Then say, **"These verses declare that Jesus is not only real and living today, but that he is the preeminent Lord over all creation—including all people. Unfortunately, not everybody believes what the Bible says. Let's take a look at what some other people in the world say about Jesus."**

Assign each group a different section of the "Jesus Who?" student sheet on page 23 of this book. Also provide blank paper and writing utensils. Tell groups to read their assigned quote, then write on their papers any evidence that would support the quote's perspective. On the back of their papers, have them write any evidence they can find in Colossians 1:15–2:10 that contradicts the quote.

Allow five to ten minutes for the groups to complete their assignments. Then have the groups come together to share their findings with the whole class. After all the groups have shared, discuss these questions:

- **Why doesn't everyone believe in Jesus?**
- **Why is it hard for so many people to trust Jesus as Lord of their lives?**
- **Besides advocating false beliefs about Jesus, what are some other ways people resist letting Jesus be Lord of their lives?**

- If the people who said these quotes examined your life, would they say you believe that Jesus is more than a good prophet or a martyr? Explain.
- Do you think Jesus is the point or main purpose for living? Why or why not?
- Is Jesus the main point of your life? Why or why not?

Conclude this activity by saying, "**Nobody follows Jesus perfectly, but there's something special about people who have made their life's goal to obey and follow Jesus in everything they do. That's the kind of person God wants each of us to be. He wants to be the point of our lives—not because he's vain or stuck-up, but because he really loves us and knows what's best for us. However, he leaves it up to each person to decide whether he or she wants Jesus to be Lord. That decision faces you today and every day. What is the point of your life today? Is it Jesus or something else?**"

Make Your Point

WORSHIP AT THE THRONE

Have students kneel around the throne they created in the "Seat of Supremacy" activity. Then ask:

- **How does it feel to kneel in front of this throne?**
- **How is kneeling a symbol of submission to Christ's authority and position in creation?**

Have them get the "My Throne" handouts they completed earlier. Then say, "**We're going to continue kneeling here for a few minutes. As we kneel, I'm going to play a song. As you listen, think about what it would mean for you to ask Jesus to come and be Lord of your life. Then, if you choose to, lay your handout down at the foot of Jesus' throne as a symbol of your decision.**

"**If you're not ready to ask Jesus to be Lord of your life right now, don't feel pressured to do this. To make it easier, I'm going to ask that you all keep your eyes closed while the song is playing. When we're finished, we'll pray together.**"

Have students close their eyes, then play the song "Hymn," by Jars of Clay, found on their CD titled *Much Afraid*. If you don't have access to that song, play another song related to God's power and authority, such as "Awesome God," by Rich Mullins.

After the song, have your group stand in a circle and join hands. Take a few minutes to pray together, acknowledging Jesus as the Lord over all creation and asking him to help your students submit their lives to him every day.

Materials needed:
Students' handouts from the "My Throne" activity; decorated throne from the "Seat of Supremacy" activity; selected CD; CD player

REFLECTING ON THE LESSON

Form pairs, and have partners take turns telling each other the way they would complete these sentences:

- **One important thing I've learned from this lesson is . . . .**
- **One thing I'll do this week to help me apply what I've learned today is . . . .**

If you have time, encourage students to tell the whole group how they completed the previous sentences. Distribute copies of **Get to the Point!**, the midweek devotional found on page 24, as your students depart. Conclude by saying, "**This week, choose to be extraordinary by taking the challenge written on your handout. Then tell us all about it next week.**"

Close with prayer.

Materials needed:
Reproducible student sheet on page 24 of this book

MY THRONE

In the box at the bottom, list all the things, people and activities that are the most important to you: your friends, your school, your appearance, your future, your sports, your hobbies, your parents and family—anything that really matters to you. Then, on the throne draw pictures or write words that represent the top five important things in your life. Put the most important thing at the top of the throne, then place the rest in order somewhere beneath.

How would your life change if you made living for Jesus your main goal in life?

JESUS WHO?

"Jesus, to succeed, had to choose martyrdom. He had been a failure in all sorts of human enterprises. One was to convert everybody to love, to turning the other cheek. He was an abysmal failure at that. He was also a failure in his more militant role—scourging the moneylenders, and so forth. He changed nothing. So, basically, the only power he had at the end was the power of abdication."—Peter A. Bien, professor of English at Dartmouth College, translator of *The Last Temptation of Christ*

"There was no such person in the history of the world as Jesus Christ. There was no historical, living, breathing, sentient human being by that name. Ever. [The Bible] is a fictional, non-historical narrative. The myth is good for business."—Jon Murray, former President of American Atheists

"Muslims see him as the greatest prophet before the prophet of Islam [Mohammed]. He is the prophet of inward spiritual life. Islam does not accept that he was crucified, died, then was resurrected. Islam believes he was taken to heaven without dying, without suffering the pain of death."—Seyyed Hossein Masr, Professor of Islamic studies at George Washington University

These quotes were excepted from *Life* magazine, December 1994.

GET TO THE POINT!

Discovering How People See You

Take this sheet with you as you go about your daily routine this week. During the week, find five people you know well and ask them to answer this question:

Based on what you see of the way I live, what would you say is the main purpose or message of my life?

Write each person's response in the space below:

1. Person: _____
Response:

2. Person: _____
Response:

3. Person: _____
Response:

4. Person: _____
Response:

5. Person: _____
Response:

After you have written all five responses, ask yourself these questions:
- **How do you feel about how people describe your purpose in life?**

- **How would _you_ describe your purpose in life?**

- **What changes would you like to make in your life so that other people see your life's purpose more clearly?**

- **What three things can you do to start making these changes this week?**

Missing the Point 3

In this session, your students will be challenged to stay focused on a task while facing several distractions at once. Then they'll explore how the distractions and struggles in their own lives can keep them from focusing on the real point of life—following Jesus. Through this exploration, your teens can discover how they can avoid missing the point of their existence every day by training themselves to focus their lives on Christ.

State Your Case

1 ANARCHY GAME

Before students arrive, place two trash cans at one end of the room. Once everyone has arrived, form two teams and give each team a stack of old newspapers. Say, **"We're going to play the famous Newspaper Game. When I say 'go,' your team will have 30 seconds to try to beat the other team. On your mark, get set, go!"**

When students hesitate or ask questions, say, **"Everybody knows the goal of the Newspaper Game! Let's do it! Ready? Go!"**

When the game fails to work a second time, ask them these questions:
- **Why doesn't the Newspaper Game make sense to you?**
- **Why is it important for you to know the point of the game I'm asking you to play?**
- **How does it feel to not understand what the point of the game is?**
- **How is that like what happens to people who don't understand the point or purpose of their lives?**
- **How is trying to play a game without knowing the point like trying to live life without understanding what life is all about?**

Close the discussion by saying, **"Loving and following Jesus is the point of life. But lots of times Christians easily lose sight of Jesus and get caught up in daily distractions and pressures, or even find themselves struggling with a particular sin or problem. Today we're going to talk about some of the most common ways we can get distracted and miss the point of living. But first let's play the Newspaper Game the way it's supposed to go."**

LESSON TEXT
Colossians 2:9-23

LESSON FOCUS
God wants us to avoid sin so we can be free.

LESSON GOALS
As a result of participating in this lesson, students will:
- Experience pressures that try to distract them from following a straight course.
- Discuss the real-life pressures and struggles that distract them from God.
- Discover how they can stay focused on Jesus regardless of life's pressures and distractions.

Materials needed:
Newspapers; two trash cans

Check This . . .
If your students took the "Get to the Point!" Challenge last week, take a few minutes at the start of the session to have them share their experience with the group.

Assign each group a different trash can. Have group members each make two or three paper wads from the newspaper and stand at least six feet from the trash can. On "go," have groups race to see which team can toss the greatest number of paper wads into their trash can in 30 seconds. When time is up, stop the action and count up the paper wads. Then congratulate the winning team.

2 STRAIGHT & NARROW

Form groups of four and give each group a roll of masking tape. Ask students to select one person from their group to be the Tape Master. Have groups each stand next to one of the walls. Then say, **"The Tape Master's task is to lay a straight line of masking tape on the floor from one end of the room to the other. The Tape Master must move any and all obstacles out of the way, staying completely focused on the task so the tape line doesn't bend to the right or left."**

Tell the rest of the group members that their job is to try to distract their Tape Master so that he or she fails to lay a straight line of tape. Group members can do anything they want to distract their Tape Master except directly block the Tape Master's path or touch him or her in any way.

Once they understand the directions, start the game. Depending on the size of the room and the number of students attending, you may have several Tape Masters crossing paths, as well as a bunch of group members making noise and jumping around creating distractions. All the chaos will only add to the effectiveness of this activity.

When the Tape Masters have finished their tape lines, use the yardstick to investigate which lines (if any) ended up perfectly straight. Then have groups discuss these questions:

- **How did it feel to try to create a straight line with so many distractions?**
- **How did it feel to create distractions for someone who was trying to achieve a specific goal?**
- **How is pursuing a goal in the midst of distractions like trying to stay focused on Jesus in daily life?**
- **What are some distractions that can keep you from focusing on Jesus?**

Conclude the discussion by saying, **"Jesus is the ultimate point of life. But we each face a lot of distractions every day. Sometimes we're distracted by temptation and sin, and sometimes we're distracted by the busyness of life. Today we're going to talk about some specific distractions and struggles we face and learn how we can avoid them."**

Cut to the Chase

1 DEMANDING DISTRACTIONS

Form four groups, possibly by asking students to choose their favorite "distraction" from among these choices: talking on the phone, participating in chat rooms online, shopping with friends or watching TV. Then assign each group one of these areas: School, Work, Home and Friends. Distribute 3" x 5" index cards and writing utensils to each person, then have students in each group work together to create a list of both good and bad things people pressure them to do in their assigned area. For example, the School group might list things like: do homework, skip class, join clubs, play sports, worry about grades, cheat on tests or play in the band.

Once all the groups have listed about 10 items, have all the groups stand and face the front of the room. On your cue, have students in each group begin to start calling out all the items on their list, repeating them over and over until you say to stop. Once all the groups are calling out items at the same time, begin to play the song "Where He Leads Me," by Twila Paris, from the CD titled *My Utmost For His Highest.* If you don't have access to that song, play a similar song that talks about the importance of following Jesus above all else.

Once the song is playing, quietly tell the groups to stop, one group at a time. When everyone is silent, ask them to close their eyes and listen to the song. After a few more minutes, lower the volume on the song, then turn it off.

Have students gather in their groups to discuss these questions:

- **How did you feel when we were all calling out the distractions and struggles that we face in everyday life?**
- **How was that chaotic experience similar to how it feels for you in real life?**
- **Did you know the song was playing in the midst of all that noise? Why or why not?**
- **What was the message of the song, once you stopped to listen to it?**
- **How is not hearing the song similar to the way we often lose sight of the point of living in our daily routine?**

Have groups read together Colossians 2:9-15. Then ask:

- **What do you think it means to "put off" the sinful nature?**
- **How can putting off the sinful nature help us stay focused on Jesus?**
- **How does focusing on Jesus and avoiding sin keep us free?**

Conclude the discussion by saying, **"Sin creates problems—problems that eventually lead to death. But God wants us to avoid sin and distractions so we can stay free and focused on what really matters in life—following Jesus."**

2 DO NOT KNOTS

Form four groups. If you did the previous option, just have students stay in their groups from that activity. Have groups each choose one volunteer to be "Joe Christian" or "Jane Christian." Give each group a supply of cloth strips and sections of rope. Tape a large sheet of newsprint to the wall, then say, **"In Colossians, Paul didn't just talk about how the sinful nature can distract us from the point of following Christ. He also talked about how other people can try to distract you by pressuring you to focus on religious rituals or traditions that may sound good at first but really have nothing to do with following Christ."**

To give students an example of what you mean, ask a few volunteers to read different parts of Colossians 2:16-23. Then ask:

- **What are some religious practices or traditions that you feel pressured to focus on, even though they don't really have any meaning to you or don't seem to help you focus on Jesus?**

Write their responses on the newsprint. Then discuss each response to determine whether it's a religious distraction or something valuable to genuine faith. To help get the discussion started, you might write down some of these controversial examples:

- Never smoke, drink or dance.
- Don't wear makeup.

Materials needed:
Bibles; cloth strips; rope; newsprint; masking tape; selected CD; CD player

Check This . . .

As you lead this activity, it's important to help your teens understand that traditions are not bad in and of themselves. On the contrary, traditions give us a way to celebrate our heritage, learn about our faith and share meaningful experiences with others. Traditions become a stumbling block only when we (or other people) try to make a tradition into a law that people must follow in order to be right with God. When that happens, the tradition can actually become a heresy or wrong belief that lures people away from the simple message of salvation that Jesus came to give.

Check This . . .

If students mention a practice you don't think belongs on the list, pause to ask these questions:

- **How does this tradition (or practice) distract you from following Jesus in freedom?**
- **How would your life be more free in Christ if you didn't have to deal with this pressure?**

Materials needed:

Bibles; writing utensils; reproducible student sheet on page 30 of this book; envelopes

- Never miss church on Sunday.
- Don't hang out with a bad crowd.
- Don't hang out with non-Christians.
- Don't listen to secular music.
- Never get angry.
- Be nice to everyone, no matter what they do to you.

Each time your group agrees that an item they've listed is a genuine modern-day religious distraction, say, **"As a symbol of the way this distraction binds up our freedom in Christ, use the cloth strips or rope segments to bind up some part of Joe or Jane Christian's body."**

Once the newsprint is fairly long and all the Joes and Janes are completely bound from head to toe, have all the groups (including the Joes and Janes) come together and form a circle of chairs. Play musical chairs while playing a song like "Look What Love Has Done," by Jaci Velasquez (from her self-titled CD), or something similar that focuses on the freedom and blessings we have in Christ. After you've played for a few minutes, stop the game and ask the Joes and Janes:

- **What does it feel like to play this game while you're all bound up?**
- **How is that like trying to live in freedom with Christ while also trying to follow a bunch of unnecessary religious rituals and traditions?**

Conclude, **"Jesus wants us to be free. And that means not only being free from sin in our lives, but also choosing not to feel pressured to follow useless traditions and practices that really do nothing to help us grow in Christ."**

FREE AT LAST!

Have students gather in a circle. Ask a volunteer to read aloud Colossians 2:9-23. Then ask:

- **How does avoiding sin in our lives keep us free?**
- **How does being free allow us to focus on what really matters in life?**
- **Why does Jesus want us to be free?**

Read the following true story to the group. As you read, ask students to think about the things in their lives that keep them from experiencing genuine freedom in Christ. Here is the story:

"In 1838, after a strong emancipation movement among blacks, slavery was abolished in Jamaica, to take effect on August 1. On the evening of the last day in July, a large company of former slaves gathered on the beach for a solemn, yet joyous, occasion. A large mahogany coffin had been constructed and placed on the sand next to an accommodating hole in the beach. All evening, the soon-to-be-emancipated slaves placed, with some ceremony, symbols of enslavement into the coffin. There were chains, leg-irons, whips, padlocks and other similar symbols of slavery. A few minutes before midnight, the box was lowered into the hole in the beach. Pushing sand into the hole to cover the coffin, all joined their voices with one accord to sing: 'Praise God from whom all blessings flow, praise him all creatures here below, praise him above ye heavenly host, praise Father, Son and Holy Ghost.' They were free from their slavery—free at last."

After the story, discuss these questions:

- **What's your reaction to this story?**

- **How is the freedom these people experienced like the freedom we experience when we become Christians?**

Distribute copies of the student sheet titled "Free at Last!" on page 30 in this book, as well as writing utensils and envelopes. Ask students to think about the questions:

- **What are some symbols of slavery that you still carry around in your**
- **In what ways do you still not feel free?**
- **How do your struggles in those areas distract you from following J**

Ask students to fill the coffin on their handout with words or pictures of that enslave them, not allowing them to experience all of the freedom Jes desires for them. Assure students that no one else will see what they ha Give them five to eight minutes to complete this task, then ask them to paper and "bury" it by sealing it in the envelope you have provided. Th their "coffins" home and keep them or dispose of them, whichever seems most appropriate.

Conclude this activity by saying, **"God wants you to be free from sin, and any other distraction that keeps you from focusing on him. That's because following Jesus is the point of life. Without Jesus, life is ultimately meaningless. Unfortunately, all the distractions and struggles we face in everyday life can cause us to miss the point completely. But it doesn't have to be that way. Jesus can help us avoid sin and other distractions so we can live free in him."**

Make Your Point

1 THE RIGHT DIRECTION

Give each student a writing utensil and a copy of the student sheet on page 31 of this book. Instruct them to silently read Colossians 2:9-23 one more time, then complete the handout. When the handouts are complete, have students form a circle. Have students read one at a time what they wrote on the center arrow. After everyone shares, encourage them to say a one-sentence prayer for the person on their right, asking God to help him or her follow through on the commitment made on the student sheet.

After the prayer, close by saying, **"God wants you to be free, so you won't ever miss the real point of life—following Jesus in everything you do. Take your handouts home and tape them on your bedroom wall as a symbol of your commitment to stay free and focused on the point."**

Materials needed:
Bibles; writing utensils; reproducible student sheet on page 31 of this book

2 REFLECTING ON THE LESSON

Form pairs, and have partners take turns telling each other the way they would complete these sentences:

- **One important thing I've learned from this lesson is . . . .**
- **One thing I'll do this week to help me apply what I've learned today is . . . .**

If you have time, encourage students to tell the whole group how they completed the previous sentences. Then distribute copies of **Get to the Point!**, the midweek devotional found on page 32, to each student. Conclude by saying, **"This week, choose to be extraordinary by taking the challenge written on your handout. Then tell us all about it next week."**

Close with prayer.

Materials needed:
Reproducible student sheet on page 32 of this book

ee at LAST!

...for you to experience real free-...sting him to take away all the things ...lave you. What are some symbols of ...ry that you still carry around in your life? In ...at ways do you still not feel free?

He invites you to give those things to him by burying them. Fill the coffin below with words or pictures of things that enslave you, not allowing you to enjoy the total freedom Jesus offers.

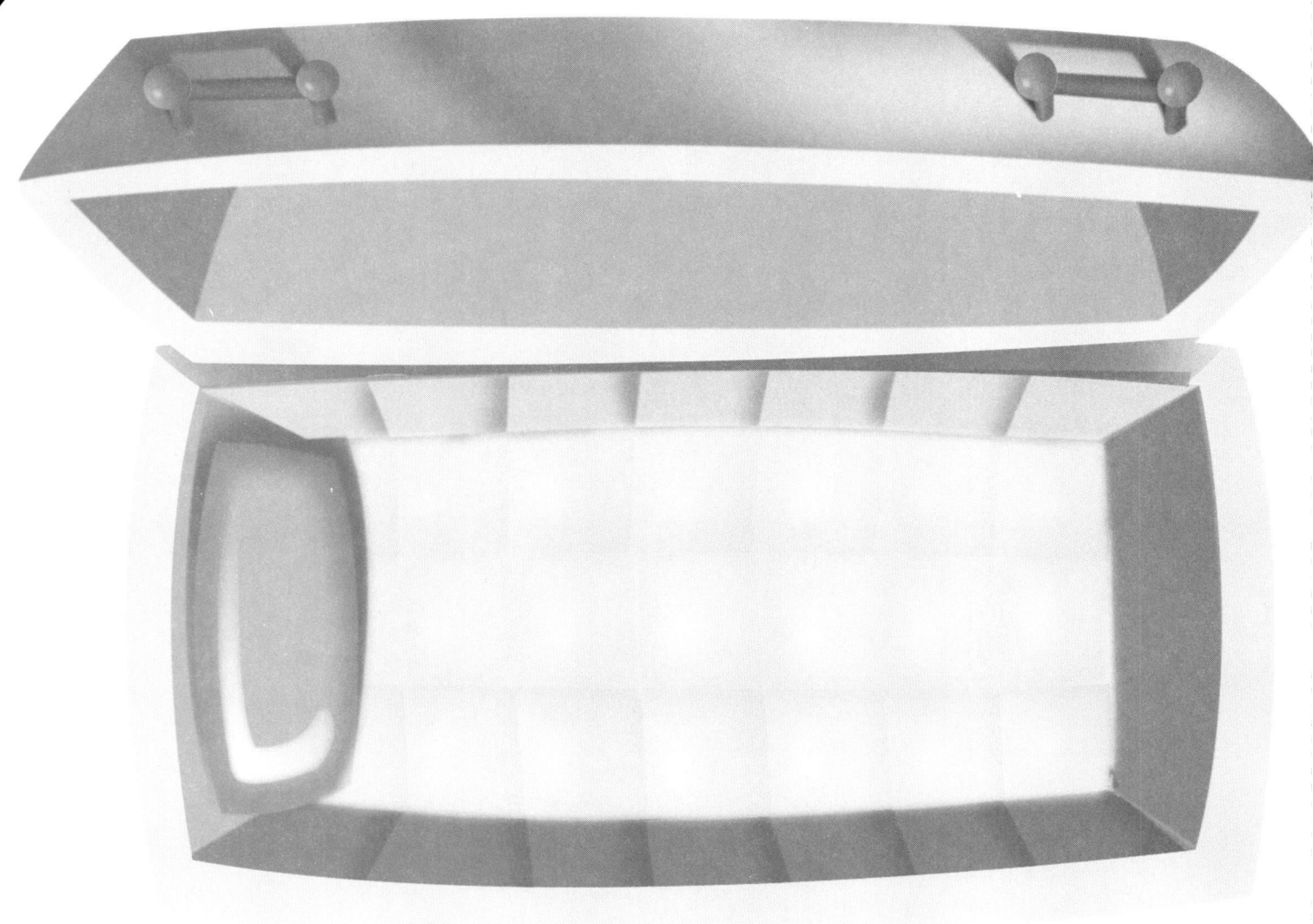

the Right Direction

Beside each of the arrows below, write one sin or distraction that keeps you from focusing on Jesus as the main point of your life. Then, in the center arrow, write one positive thing you can do to avoid these sins and distractions in the coming week.

GET TO THE POINT!

Where I Miss It

When you get home, place this sheet and a pen next to your bed. Then, every night this week, just before you go to sleep, write down all the things that occupied your time and your thoughts during the day. At the end of the week, review what you wrote and see if you can discover any sins or other distractions that regularly keep you from following Jesus in all that you do. For example, maybe you spend a lot of time worrying about your grades. Or maybe you focus so much on what your friends think of you that you lose sight of Jesus' love for you and his guidance in your life.

In the last box at the bottom of the page, write a letter to Jesus, telling him about the things that distract you and asking him to help you be free from sin and distraction so you can focus on loving and following him with all your heart, every day.

Day 1

Day 2

Day 3

Day 4

Day 5

Day 6

Day 7

Dear Jesus:

Seeking the Point 4

In this session, your students will play a game in which they'll try to keep their focus on two different things at once. Then they'll creatively explore what Paul meant when he said that our lives are "hidden in Christ" and that we should set our minds on the "things above" where Christ is. Through this exploration, your group can learn how to experience true meaning in life by seeking the things above and not focus their energies on things in the world.

State Your Case

1 PLAY DEAD

Once everyone arrives, form trios. Ask one person in each group to lay on the floor and play dead to the best of his or her ability—that is, no movement, no smiling or laughing and no peeking. Ask the other two members of each trio to do everything they can (short of actually touching the person) to get their "dead" member to show some signs of life. They can try to make their "dead" person laugh, gently blow on his or her face—anything that doesn't involve touching.

Have trio members switch roles a few times so that all the students get a chance to play dead. After the experience, have trios discuss the question, **"What was hard about playing dead?"**

Read aloud Colossians 3:1-4, then ask:
- **What do you think these verses mean when they say we are "dead"?**
- **How is playing dead in this activity like dying to ourselves and trying to set our minds on things above?**
- **Why is it hard to focus on things above and not on earthly things?**
- **Do you think God's command is unreasonable? Why or why not?**
- **Do you think God's command is impossible? Why or why not?**

Close the discussion by saying, **"God did not tell us to focus on him and things above just to frustrate us. Even though God's command is difficult, obeying it is the only way we can experience true abundant life. That's because true life is hidden in Jesus Christ—and nowhere else."**

LESSON TEXT
Colossians 3:1-4

LESSON FOCUS
True life is hidden in Christ—and nowhere else.

LESSON GOALS
As a result of participating in this lesson, students will:
- Experience what it's like to try to focus on two things at once.
- Explore what it means to set their minds on the "things above."
- Discover specific ways they can set their minds on Christ every day.

Check This . . .
If your students took the "Get to the Point!" Challenge last week, take a few minutes at the start of the session to have them share their experience with the group.

Check This . . .
A great song to help introduce this session is "You," recorded by Jaci Velasquez on her self-titled album. The song "Worlds Apart," by Jars of Clay, also fits well with this study. It is recorded on their self-titled release.

Materials needed:
Bibles; a bag of M&M candies or something similar

2 HIDDEN TREATS

Before students arrive, hide a bag of treats somewhere in the room. Make it as difficult for them to find as possible. Once everyone arrives, tell your group you've hidden a bag of treats and challenge them to find it. Allow them to search for up to five minutes, giving hints only when they seem frustrated enough to give up. Once the candy is found, allow all the students to share it. Then ask:

- **What was your reaction to having to look for the candy?**
- **How is that like the reaction people sometimes have to seeking God?**
- **Did you get frustrated on your search? Why or why not?**
- **Did you feel like giving up? Why or why not?**
- **How is that like the way we feel at times as we try to understand and follow Jesus?**
- **How is Jesus like this hidden treasure?**
- **Why do you think Jesus chooses to be hidden in this way?**

Conclude by reading aloud Colossians 3:1-4, then saying, "**Jesus is hidden, sort of like this candy was. But this passage says that life—true life—is also hidden with him. That's why God wants us to seek Jesus with all of our hearts, and not to dwell on earthly things. Today we're going to explore what it means to 'set your hearts on things above, where Christ is.'**"

Cut to the Chase

1 CROSS EYES

Form groups of five or fewer, possibly by the different schools your students attend. Instruct each group to search their personal items for the two most expensive things they possess as a group. For example, a watch, a necklace, a Bible or even a pair of shoes. Have groups place one item at one end of the room and the other item at the opposite end of the room. Then have groups each choose one volunteer to be the guardian of these treasures. Tell the rest of the group members that their job is to test their guardian by trying to steal their group treasures without being touched by the guardian. Tell the guardians they can protect the treasures only by touching anyone who comes near them. If touched, group members must step away and wait 30 seconds before trying again.

Start the test. After a minute (or after the guardian loses both of the treasures), have the group choose a new guardian. Continue until everyone has had a chance to be the guardian. After the experience, have groups discuss these questions:

- **What's your reaction to this experience?**
- **Why was it hard to guard two items at once?**
- **How did you deal with that challenge?**

Have groups read together Colossians 3:1-4 again, then discuss:

- **How was trying to guard these two items like trying to focus on the "things above" and on "earthly things" at the same time?**
- **Why does God want us to focus on the things above and not on earthly things?**
- **How do you focus on earthly things?**
- **How do you focus on things above?**
- **What do you think would happen to you if you really did always focus only**

Materials needed:
Bibles

Check This . . .
Some teens may have a hard time believing that their lives would be abundant if they focused everything on Christ. That's because young people (and adults) often have an image of godliness that looks pretty boring to them—people sitting around praying and reading their Bibles all day, then going to church every night. If you sense you have some students who share this perspective, ask them these questions:

- **When Jesus said he came to give abundant life, what do you think he meant?**
- **Do you think the Christian life is the most abundant, most exciting way to live? Why or why not?**
- **If Jesus said our lives in him would be complete and abundant, but that's not what we're experiencing, where does the problem lie?**
- **What can we do to find out whether Jesus is telling the truth?**

on the things above? only on earthly things?

Conclude the discussion by saying, **"True life is hidden in Christ—not here on earth. That's why God wants us to focus everything in our lives on Christ. He wants us to have abundant life, and he knows we won't find it anywhere else."**

2 HIGH AND LOW

Place a sheet of newsprint on the ceiling—or at least high on a wall.

Place another sheet of newsprint on the floor. On the high newsprint, write "Things Above." On the low newsprint, write "Things Below."

Form two groups and have each group read together Colossians 3:1-4 again. Then ask one group to write examples of the "things above" that we should focus on in life to please God. Ask the other group to write examples of the "things below" that often distract us or tempt us to lose sight of Jesus.

After each group has listed 10 or more items, gather everyone together and ask volunteers to explain why their group wrote the things they did. Encourage students to add more items to either list as they come up in the discussion. Then discuss these questions:

- **Was it easy to come up with items for your list? Why or why not?**
- **Why is it often easier to come up with things that distract us from Jesus rather than things that would draw us to focus on him?**
- **How hard is it to write items on the ceiling versus writing them on the floor?**
- **How is that like the difficulty of focusing our attention on things above instead of the earthly things we've listed here?**
- **Why didn't God make it easy for us to focus our lives on him?**
- **Why does God want us to focus on Jesus, even though it's harder than focusing on the world?**

Conclude, **"God wants us to focus our hearts and minds on the things above because he knows this secret about life: True life is hidden in Christ—and nowhere else. Of course, we can find excitement and thrills in other places, but all of these things below are temporary and fleeting. Pursuing them will not fulfill the desire of our hearts in a way that lasts. But Jesus brings abundant life that is eternal. It never ends. That's why he wants us to seek him, like a hidden treasure, so we can experience true life that lasts."**

Materials needed:
Bibles; newsprint; masking tape; markers

3 HIDDEN!

If you haven't already done so, read aloud Colossians 3:1-4 for the whole group. Then say, **"I'm going to ask you a big question about this passage. It's a hard question, a challenging question. But I think you're up to it. When I give you the question, think about it, then answer it the best you can."** Give each student a writing utensil and a copy of the student sheet on page 38 of this book. Allow three to five minutes for them to study the question and answer it to the best of their ability.

When time is up, have several volunteers share what they wrote as the answer to the question. Congratulate them on their insight. Then say, **"Let's see if this item I brought can help provide us with more insight into what it means for our life to be 'hidden' in Christ."**

Bring out a plant and a trash bag large enough to cover it. Ask: **"What would**

Materials needed:
Bibles; writing utensils; the reproducible student sheet on page 38 of this book; a plant with a black trash bag large enough to cover it

happen to this plant if I pulled it up by the roots? Why?"

Place a black trash bag over the plant. Then ask, "**What would happen if I left the plant under the bag for a long time? Why?**"

Have two volunteers read Psalm 1:1-3 and 1 John 1:5-7. Then ask:

- **How is this plant's relationship with the soil and the light like our relationship with Christ?**
- **How is the plant's life "hidden" in the soil and light?**
- **How is that like the way our life is "hidden" in Christ, even though we're living down here on earth?**

Comment, "**The plant's life comes from the light and the soil. It cannot really live without them. In the same way, true life for us comes from our connection with Christ. Focusing our lives on Jesus gives us life in the same way this plant gets life from growing roots in the soil and pointing its leaves toward the sun.**"

Ask:

- **Based on this analogy, what do you think happens to our lives when we don't focus on Jesus, but dwell on earthly things?**
- **What are some of the earthly things that most often distract you from God?**
- **What are some ways you can focus your lives on Jesus more in the coming week?**

Conclude, "**For each of us, true life is hidden in Christ. That's why it's so important to focus our hearts and minds on him every day, and avoid getting caught up in earthly things.**"

Make Your Point

1 WALK IN THE LIGHT

Set out a large candle and light it, then have students gather around it in a circle. Give each person a smaller candle. Then turn off the lights and say, "**This candle in the middle represents Jesus. Each of these candles represents our lives before we met Jesus. Without the light of Christ, we have no light of our own. We're like unlit candles.**"

Place your candlewick into the "Jesus" flame, then say, "**But by seeking the life that is hidden in Christ, his light is revealed in us.**"

Hold up your now-lit candle, and read aloud 1 John 1:5-7. Then say, "**If you want to know the abundant eternal life that's hidden in Christ, do what I have done, as a symbol of your desire.**"

Allow students to take turns using the Jesus candle to light their own flames.

Distribute writing utensils and copies of the student sheet on page 39 titled "Walk in the Light." Close the session by listening to the song "Live the Life," by Michael W. Smith on his *Live the Life* CD or "In the Light," recorded by dc Talk on their album titled *Jesus Freak*. As students listen to the song you choose, let them record their responses to the questions on the student sheet.

After the song is over, conclude by asking God to permeate your students' hearts with his awesome light and then to open doors for them to share his light with others.

2 REFLECTING ON THE LESSON

Form pairs, and have partners take turns telling each other the way they would complete these sentences:

- **One important thing I've learned from this lesson is . . . .**
- **One thing I'll do this week to help me apply what I've learned today is . . . .**

If you have time, encourage students to tell the whole group how they completed the previous sentences. Then distribute copies of **Get to the Point!**, the midweek devotional found on page 40, to each student. Conclude by saying, **"This week, choose to be extraordinary by taking the challenge written on your handout. Then tell us all about it next week."**

Close with prayer.

Materials needed:
Reproducible student sheet on page 40 of this book

Hidden!

"Since, then, you have been raised with Christ, set your hearts on things above, where Christ is seated at the right hand of God. Set your minds on things above, not on earthly things. For you died, and your life is now hidden with Christ in God. When Christ, who is your life, appears, then you also will appear with him in glory."—Colossians 3:1-4

How can you be hidden with Christ in God and here in this room at the same time?

Walk in the Light

"This is the message we have heard from him and declare to you: God is light; in him there is no darkness at all. If we claim to have fellowship with him yet walk in the darkness, we lie and do not live by the truth. But if we walk in the light, as he is in the light, we have fellowship with one another, and the blood of Jesus, his Son, purifies us from all sin."—1 John 1:5-7

As you listen to the song, answer these questions:

- What is the singer saying is our responsibility?

- How can you be sure you are living in the light with Jesus?

- St. Francis of Assisi once said, "Preach the gospel to all the world and if necessary, use words." What are some practical ways in which you could share the light with your friends?

With your family?

With your neighbors?

GET TO THE POINT!

Live the Life

In the space below, list three ways you can practically focus on the things above this week—one that you can do while you're alone, one that involves your family and one that involves your friends. For example, you could:

1. Spend 15 minutes praying and reading your Bible every day this week.
2. Do something nice for your parents that they don't expect. For example, tell them each one thing you love about them or clean the house without being asked.
3. Pray every day for your friends, asking God to help them focus on the things above and avoid earthly things.

1. _____
_____
_____
_____
_____

2. _____
_____
_____
_____

3. _____
_____
_____
_____

Once you've chosen your three things, pick a time and a place to carry out each challenge in the coming week. When you've accomplished all three, write your feelings about what you've done in the space below.

Making Your Point Every Day

In this session, your students will create symbols that represent each of the qualities they're instructed to put on in Colossians 3:5–4:6. Then they'll creatively discuss why these qualities and behaviors are important to life and how they demonstrate in practical ways the real point of life—loving and following Jesus. Through this study, your teens will discover the practical ways they can focus their lives on Christ and avoid getting caught up in things that don't matter.

State Your Case

1 FRUIT ROOTS

Once everyone has arrived, give each person a piece of fruit. While they are enjoying the treat, ask students to tell all they know about the plant the fruit came from. For example, grapes come from vines that must be cultivated for years before they begin to bear good fruit, while bananas grow in abundance from trees in tropical regions.

After your group members have shared all they know about each fruit's origin, ask:
- **How is it that you know these bananas came from a banana tree?**
- **Would you believe me if I told you these bananas came from a grapevine or a berry bush? Why not?**
- **What does this saying mean to you: "A tree is known by its fruit"?**
- **How are we like fruit-bearing trees?**

Say, **"In the same way that we can tell a lot about a tree by looking at its fruit, we can also tell a lot about a person by looking at the 'fruit' of his or her life. Today we're going to talk about what that 'fruit' is and what kind of 'fruit' we want others to see in us."**

2 RESTRICTIVE CLOTHING

Tape a sheet of newsprint to the wall and title it "Put Off." When students arrive, have them read together Colossians 3:5-11, then call out all the things the passage instructs them to "put to death," "rid" themselves of or "put off." Have a student volunteer write their responses on the newsprint. (If they have trouble coming up with items, use this list to help them out: *sexual immorality,*

LESSON TEXT
Colossians 3:5–4:6

LESSON FOCUS
God gives us practical ways to live out the point of life every day.

LESSON GOALS
As a result of participating in this lesson, students will:
- Explore what it means to "put off" certain behaviors listed in Colossians 3:5–4:6.
- Discover how they can "put on" behaviors and qualities every day that help them focus on Jesus.
- Learn the importance of demonstrating the point of life regardless of how they feel or who they're with.

Materials needed:
A basket of assorted fruit

Check This . . .
If your students took the "Get to the Point!" Challenge last week, take a few minutes at the start of the session to have them share their experience with the group.

Materials needed:
Newsprint; masking tape; markers; several coats; a dictionary

impurity, lust, evil desires, greed, anger and rage, malice, slander, filthy language and *lying*.)

Call another volunteer to the front of the room. For each item listed, have the volunteer put on a separate jacket—one jacket on top of the next, so that the volunteer begins to look "stuffed." If some of the jackets won't fit, just drape them over the shoulders and tie them around the neck, or let the volunteer tie them around his or her waist. Once all the jackets are on, ask the volunteer to accomplish some simple tasks—for example, tie his or her shoes, give other group members a hug or scratch his or her back.

Give several students dictionaries and have them each look up a different word from the list they created. As the definition of each word is read, take one of the jackets off the volunteer and toss it on the floor. After all the definitions are read, have the volunteer sit down and read again Colossians 3:5-11. Then ask the volunteer:

- **How did it feel to wear all these jackets?**
- **Were you able to do the tasks I asked of you? Why or why not?**

Ask the whole group:

- **How is wearing these jackets like "putting on" all these negative behaviors and attitudes in real life?**
- **How do attitudes and behaviors like those listed in these verses keep us from living in real freedom?**

Say, **"God wants us to live in total freedom. But he knows we can do that only if we learn to focus on Jesus in everyday life. And that means putting off negative attitudes and behaviors like those we've just mentioned, and then clothing ourselves in the attributes of Christ. Today we're going to talk about some of these practical ways we can focus our lives on the main point—Jesus Christ."**

Cut to the Chase

DECORATED CHRISTIANS

Materials needed:
Bibles; pipe cleaners; masking tape; newsprint; marker

Check This . . .
If some students don't understand the meaning of some of the words listed in the passage, use the dictionaries you used earlier to give them a clearer idea of what they mean.

Form pairs and give each pair a few pipe cleaners. Have pairs read Colossians 3:12–4:6, then have students call out all the qualities and behaviors listed in the passage that Christians are supposed to do daily as a practical way to demonstrate their devotion to Jesus. List their responses on newsprint. Specific qualities listed in the text include: *compassion, kindness, humility, gentleness, patience, forbearance, forgiveness, love, peace, thankfulness, God's Word, wisdom, singing psalms, hymns and spiritual songs, submission, obedience, sincerity, commitment to work, fairness, prayer* and *grace.*

Assign each pair one or more words from the list you created, and ask them to use their pipe cleaners to create a symbol that represents that attitude or behavior. For example, for compassion they might create a heart. If they can't think of a symbol, just have them shape their pipe cleaner into the first letter of their assigned word—but push their creativity first!

When all the pairs are finished, ask a volunteer to come stand in front of the whole group. One at a time, have pairs come up and "decorate" the volunteer by taping their pipe cleaner creation to his or her clothing. After each symbol is taped on, ask the group:

- **What's one way people would be able to see this attitude or behavior lived out in your daily life?**

Write their responses on newsprint, next to the appropriate quality or behavior listed on the newsprint. When all the pairs have finished, discuss these questions:

- **How does our volunteer look?**
- **If he or she went to school this way, what do you think people would say?**
- **How is that like or unlike the way people would react if, instead of just wearing these symbols, we were to really do the things each symbol represented?** (To help your students answer this question, refer to the information recorded next to each word on the newsprint list.)

Say, **"True life is found in Jesus; he is the point we should focus on each day. These qualities and behaviors we've listed give us practical ways we can do that every day. If we were to put on each of these qualities every day, not only would our lives be transformed, but we would also powerfully impact the lives of the people we interact with on a daily basis."**

Point to the newsprint and ask, **"Is this the way you want to live? Why or why not?"**

Conclude, **"We all have a long way to go to fulfilling all the commands on this list. But we may have come farther than we think. Let's take a minute to point out which of these qualities we already see in one another."**

2 I SEE YOUR POINT!

Give each person a writing utensil and a copy of the student sheet on page 46 of this book. Have students write their names at the top of the certificates, then pass them in to you. Mix up the papers, then redistribute them, making sure students don't get their own certificates. Ask them not to let anyone see whose certificate they got. Caution: You may need to jump in with some positive traits for a particular student if someone seems to be struggling with things to write. Especially be alert to help new or shy students.

Once everyone has a certificate, say, **"Complete this certificate for the person whose name is at the top. Write in some of the real-life qualities and behaviors you see in that person, based on Colossians 3:12–4:6 and the newsprint list we created. Do not put your name anywhere on the certificate, and do not let anyone else see whose certificate you have."**

Once they finish the certificates, instruct them to return them to you. Once you have received about half the certificates, begin taping them to the wall, mixing up the order so students can't easily guess who filled theirs out. Once all the certificates are completed and on the wall, direct students to find their own certificate and read it. Then get their attention by asking:

- **How does it feel to be recognized and known by your fruit?**
- **Is this the kind of fruit you hoped others might see in you? Why or why not?**
- **Do you think you bear this kind of fruit with everyone you know, or just around certain people or at certain times? Explain.**
- **Why is it so important that we each focus on bearing the right kind of fruit in our lives all the time—regardless of where we are or who we are with?**

Conclude the discussion by saying, **"Through this study, we can see that God has shown us specific, practical ways we can focus our hearts and minds on things above—that is, on Jesus—every day."**

Materials needed:
Bibles; writing utensils; masking tape; reproducible certificate on page 46 of this book

Check This . . .
A great song to play while students are completing their certificates is "Universe Next Door," by Wes King. The song is recorded on his CD titled *A Room Full of Stories*. Another possibility is "Call Me Christian" recorded by Smalltown Poets on their *Listen Closely* release.

MODELS OF PERFECTION

Ahead of time, you will need to make a copy of the reproducible student sheet titled "Models of Perfection" on an overhead transparency. Form five groups and give each group a writing utensil and a copy of the reproducible sheet on page 47 of this book. Assign each group one of these passages: Colossians 3:5-11; 3:12-14; 3:15-17; 3:18–4:1; and 4:2-6. Then say, **"Based on your assigned passage, write down some of the traits of a person who lives out the commands in your passage. You will write these characteristics next to the guy and girl models on your handout. For example, if your passage says the person has compassion, then write one or two ways that person would demonstrate compassion in daily life—by listening to people, helping those in need and so on. And you will write these ways to show compassion near the models' hands. If your passage says to put to death lust and evil desires, you will write that near the brain of one of the models. When you're finished with your description of a godly model, you'll share it with the whole group."**

Allow groups five minutes to complete their assignment, then have groups each share their descriptions. As they do so, write them on your overhead transparency and project it on the wall for all to see. After all the descriptions have been shared, ask:

- **Would you like to be friends with a person who demonstrated all of the qualities we just listed? Why or why not?**
- **Do you know anybody like this? Is it possible to live out these characteristics perfectly?**
- **If you did know someone like this, what would you say is the point of his or her life?**
- **What does God say is the point of each of our lives?**
- **How do you feel knowing that this is the kind of person God wants you to be?**
- **On a scale of 1 to 10, with 10 being perfection, how close do you think you are to being this kind of person? Explain.**
- **What's one way you can begin to become more like this person this week?**

Close the discussion by saying, **"God wants us to focus our lives on him because he knows that's the only way we'll ever know true, abundant life. And in this passage, he shows us specifically what a life focused on Jesus looks like in the real world."**

Make Your Point

REAL-WORLD CONNECTIONS

Have students form a circle. Direct their attention to the newsprint list they created earlier and encourage them to silently choose one positive quality they want God to help them build into their lives. When everyone has chosen a quality, say, **"Let's close today by praying for each other, asking God to help us each focus our hearts and minds on him in practical ways—ways that bear fruit other people can see."**

Lead students in praying together by having each person take turns saying aloud the quality he or she wants to develop. After each person speaks, ask students to pray silently for 15 seconds or so for that person's request. Then ask the

Materials needed:
Bibles; reproducible student sheet on page 47 of this book; writing utensils; overhead transparency; marker; overhead projector

Materials needed:
Newsprint lists from earlier activities

next person to share his or her request. Continue until everyone in the circle has been prayed for.

REFLECTING ON THE LESSON

Form pairs, and have partners take turns telling each other the way they would complete these sentences:

Materials needed:
Reproducible student sheet on page 48 of this book

- **One important thing I've learned from this lesson is . . . .**
- **One thing I'll do this week to help me apply what I've learned today is . . . .**

If you have time, encourage students to tell the whole group how they completed the previous sentences. Distribute copies of **Get to the Point!**, the midweek devotional found on page 48, to each student. Conclude by saying, **"This week, choose to be extraordinary by taking the challenge written on your handout. Then tell us all about it next week."**

Close with prayer.

I See Your Point!

In support of my brothers and sisters in Christ, and their efforts to focus on Jesus as the one true point of their lives, I hereby present this certificate of appreciation to

_____ in recognition of the outstanding, awesome, godly qualities I see demonstrated in practical ways in his or her life. Among these are:

_____, in light of these positive qualities, I do hereby offer my
(name)
thanks and appreciation for your efforts to focus on Jesus as the point of your life. I can see Jesus in you. Congratulations!

MoDEls oF PeRfeCtiOn

Your group's Bible passage is:

Write down some of the traits of a person who lives out the commands in your passage next to the guy and girl models below. For example, if your passage says the person has compassion, then write one or two ways that person would demonstrate compassion in daily life—by listening to people, helping those in need and so on. Write these ways to show compassion near the models' hands. If your passage says to put to death lust and evil desires, you will write that near the brain of one of the models.

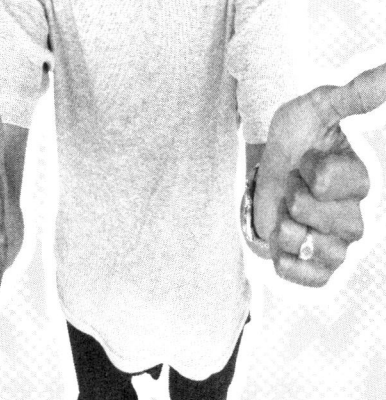

Do you know anybody like this?

Is it possible to live out these characteristics perfectly?

If not, what should be our goal?

What's one way you can begin to become more like this person this week?

GET TO THE POINT!

Point-of-Life Personal Profile

Ask two or three of your most trusted friends or family members to complete this survey of the positive qualities they see in you. Then use the information they provide to direct your prayers and efforts to bear good fruit for Jesus in your life.

Place a check mark next to each quality or behavior below that you regularly see lived out in _____'s (insert your name) life.

- ❏ doesn't lie
- ❏ treats others with gentleness
- ❏ is kind
- ❏ doesn't give in to anger or rage
- ❏ is humble
- ❏ abstains from sex before marriage
- ❏ loves easily
- ❏ doesn't talk badly about others behind their backs
- ❏ is patient
- ❏ shows compassion to others
- ❏ is sincere
- ❏ has a rich prayer life
- ❏ tells others about Jesus
- ❏ treats others fairly

- ❏ avoids using filthy language
- ❏ forgives easily
- ❏ studies God's Word regularly
- ❏ encourages others to follow God
- ❏ is not greedy
- ❏ is committed to doing his or her best
- ❏ seems peaceful
- ❏ puts up with others even when they're crabby
- ❏ avoids sexual temptation
- ❏ values wisdom
- ❏ isn't out to get anyone
- ❏ obeys authority
- ❏ has a thankful attitude
- ❏ _____ (other)

Sharing the Point 6

In this session, your students will work within a team to carry an important message to people who need to hear it. Then they'll share unique qualities they see in each other that could be used to encourage and strengthen other Christians. Through these experiences, your teens will discover how they can encourage one another to focus their lives on Jesus every day

State Your Case

1 LEAN ON THE TEAM

Once everyone has arrived, form teams of five or six, possibly by offering several options of teams or clubs you know your teens have joined (or wanted to join). These might include baseball, softball, soccer, swimming, debate, basketball, drama, German, etc. Once students are in teams, begin by saying, **"Without using chairs, tables, a wall, the floor or any other prop, work with your team to find a way you can all relax and rest at the same time by either reclining or sitting on one another."**

Allow groups a few minutes to decide how they can accomplish this task. If some groups seem stuck, consider suggesting these ideas:

- Have the group stand in a tight circle, face clockwise, then all sit down at the same time.
- Have the group stand in a tight circle, face outward, then have everyone move their feet away from the circle and lean back against one another.
- Have the team stand in a tight circle, join hands, then lean back.

Once each group has come up with an idea, ask the other groups to evaluate it:

- **Does it really involve depending on each other?**
- **Does it really allow group members to rest?**

Congratulate all the teams on their efforts. Then gather everyone together and ask:

- **What was interesting to you about this activity?**
- **Were you comfortable depending on someone else for your stability and safety? Why or why not?**
- **How is finding ways to lean or rest on each other like the way God might want us to relate to other Christians?**

LESSON TEXT
Colossians 4:7-18

LESSON FOCUS
God wants us to follow Jesus together with others.

LESSON GOALS
As a result of participating in this lesson, students will:

- Experience how it feels to work as a team to accomplish a goal.
- Discover unique qualities each of them can use to help others.
- Explore how they can encourage one another every day to focus on Christ.

Check This . . .
If your students took the "Get to the Point!" Challenge last week, take a few minutes at the start of the session to have them share their experience with the group.

Check This . . .
Several songs that deal with today's topic include "One Voice," recorded by the O. C. Supertones on their *Chase the Sun* release; "Brothers Keeper," by the Gotee Brothers on their project titled *Erace*; and "Everything (Apron Full of Stains)," on the album *Better Than This,* by The Normals.

Say, "God wants us to follow Jesus as the point of our lives. But he never intended that we do it alone. He wants us to walk out our faith in the company and support of other Christians. Today we're going to explore what it takes to really function as a part of God's team, which the Bible calls the body of Christ."

2 SPEAKING FOR GOD

Ask your students to think about one of the most important people in their lives, recalling how they know him or her and why he or she is so important to them. After a minute or two, tell them they're going to tell the rest of the group about their important person—but not in the usual way.

Form groups of four. Then say, "**Instead of telling everyone yourself, whisper all the information to your group members, then have them work together to tell all of us what you said.**"

After a few minutes, have the groups relay the information each of their members shared. After all the groups have shared, have students discuss these questions in their groups of four:

- How did it feel to relay your information through other people?
- Why is this harder than relaying the information yourself?
- Why was it important for your group to listen carefully and relay the information accurately?
- How is this experience like the way God works with us to tell the world about Jesus?
- Why is it important that we all listen and work together as a team to get the message across to the world?

Conclude this activity by saying, "**God wants our lives to reflect Jesus to the world around us. But he never intended for us to carry that message alone. He's provided other Christians for us to know, encourage and work together with to share the point of life with the world—that true life comes from loving and following Jesus. Today we're going to explore what it means to work together to carry God's message to the world.**"

Cut to the Chase

1 CARRYING THE MESSAGE

Materials needed:
Several pieces of poster board; hole punch; markers; string

Form groups of five or six. (If you did option 1 for the opening, have students stay in their groups for this activity.) Then say, "**Based on all we've studied in Colossians and all you know about God's love and salvation, work with your team to write what you think is the point or purpose of life for every person God has created.**"

Allow groups a few minutes to complete their assignments. Then have groups share what they wrote, offering any suggestions on how they might alter their statement if needed. Then say, "**Each of us is supposed to live out this point every day of our lives. And we're supposed to share this point with others and encourage them to live it. But the truth is we can't do all that alone. We need each other to get the job done. Let's do an activity to help us see why that is so.**"

Give each group two pieces of poster board, a marker and enough string to make a sandwich board. You will need to go around with the hole punch to help them complete this. Have each group choose one person to wear the "point" they created as a placard that can be read from the front and the back when their volunteer is walking. (Instruct them to choose someone who is relatively light in weight, and not wearing a dress.) Then say, **"We've got to take our message to the streets, but your message bearer can't do it alone. Your job as a group is to carry your message bearer to the street curb outside, where he or she will proclaim the 'point' as loudly as possible. To make sure all the members of your team get involved, you may not carry the message bearer on your back or shoulders, and you must not let any part of your message bearer touch the ground until you reach the curb."**

Once the message bearers reach the curb, have them yell out what's written on their billboards to the passing cars and pedestrians. Then have groups carry the message bearers back to the meeting room.

Once everyone has returned and has settled down from this wild activity, have students respond to these questions:

- **What was it like to carry your message bearer as a team?**
- **How did it feel to be carried to the curb? to yell out the "point" of life?**
- **How does this experience demonstrate the way the body of Christ should work?**
- **Why does God want us to depend on each other? to help and encourage each other?**

Say, **"When you really live for Jesus and make him the 'point' of your life, you will always have some people who reject and persecute you. But God has given each of us a body of believers to join with. God wants us to encourage each other and work together to share Jesus with the world."**

TEAM PLAYERS

Have students stay in their groups from the previous activity. Distribute writing utensils and copies of the student sheet on page 54 to each student. Then play the song "One Voice," by the O. C. Supertones. It is recorded on their album *Chase the Sun.* Ask groups to listen to the song and record their answers to the questions on the handout. After the song has been played, instruct students to share their responses. Then have them read Colossians 4:7-18 in their groups and discuss the questions at the bottom of the handout.

Once groups have discussed the last question, ask them to work together as a team to present their ideas to the rest of the class. For example, they could say their answers in unison, do a tag-team presentation or even create a quick skit to convey the information.

After the presentations, conclude, **"Working together and supporting each other is both challenging and fun. And when it comes to following Jesus, working on a team with other Christians is the best way to go."**

Materials needed:
Bibles; reproducible student sheet on page 54 of this book; writing utensils; selected CD; CD player

BLESSING CIRCLE

Have students form a circle, then read aloud Colossians 4:7-18 if you haven't already done so. Ask:

- **Why do you think Paul spoke so highly of his friends in this passage?**
- **Do you think it's important that we encourage one another by talking about each other the way that Paul did? Why or why not?**

Materials needed:
Bibles

Because this activity can be so emotionally impacting for teens, make sure you allow ample time for them to share. If your group is large and your time is limited, consider forming several "blessing circles," each comprised of six to eight group members. If any of your students brought a visitor to the group, make sure you keep them together. (You will need to be ready with some encouraging words for new or less popular teens.)

Materials needed:
Bibles; writing utensils; reproducible student sheets on pages 15, 55 of this book; colored card stock; scissors

Say, "**The point of life is to love and follow Jesus. But to do that well, we need each other. We need to be confronted when we do something wrong. But, even more, we need to be encouraged when we're doing our best. We need to know that other people see the good things in us. Let's share those good things now.**"

Ask a volunteer to come and sit in the center of the circle. Ask the rest of your group to take turns telling the center person ways they see him or her living for Jesus and loving other people in everyday life. Each time someone shares, have the center person turn his or her chair toward that person and look him or her in the eyes. Allow up to five people to share their impressions with the center person, then ask a new volunteer to come sit in the center chair. Continue this process until everyone has had a turn in the center chair.

After the activity, say, "**This is a big part of what teamwork in God's kingdom is all about. Jesus is the point of life for each of us. But we need each other to help us to stay focused on Jesus and to live for him every day.**"

Make Your Point

1 A FOCUSED LIFE

Comment, "**One way Paul encouraged his friend Archippus was to challenge him to finish the work God had given him to do. That's what I want to do with you now too. In the first session of this study, you wrote a personal dream for your life based on what you knew about God's will at that time. Let's look at those dreams we wrote, and see how we might change them now that we've reached the end of our study of Colossians.**"

Give each student a writing utensil and tell all of them to find their "My Point Exactly" student sheet completed during the first lesson in this series and taped on the wall. Have students read what they wrote and change it in any way they wish. If some students weren't present for the first session, or you didn't do that activity, simply give them a copy of the "My Point Exactly" student sheet on page 15 of this book, then have them complete the handout at this time.

When everyone is finished, say, "**Now let's take our dreams and make them reality.**"

You will want to make sufficient copies of the reproducible bookmarks on page 55 of this book ahead of time. If possible, photocopy the bookmarks onto thick, bright-colored card stock. Distribute the copies and ask students to choose and cut out their favorite design of the bookmarks. Once they have all chosen, instruct them to write on the back of the bookmark two or three ways they will change their beliefs and behavior to fulfill their personal dreams and focus their lives more on Jesus every day. When they finish, have several volunteers share what they wrote. Then say, "**Take your personal dream sheet home and place it where you can see it often. Also take home your bookmark. Place it in your Bible or some other book you read often. Let it be a reminder to keep your heart and mind focused on the real point of life—following Jesus.**"

Close with prayer, asking God to help your teens always focus on Jesus as the point of their lives.

REFLECTING ON THE LESSON

Form pairs, and have partners take turns telling each other the way they would complete these sentences:

- **One important thing I've learned from this lesson is . . . .**
- **One thing I'll do this week to help me apply what I've learned today is . . . .**

If you have time, encourage students to tell the whole group how they completed the previous sentences. Close in prayer, then distribute copies of **Get to the Point!**, the midweek devotional found on page 56, as your students depart.

Materials needed:
Reproducible student sheet on page 56 of this book

TEAM PLAYERS

As you listen to the song, "One Voice," by the O. C. Supertones, answer these questions:

• Why does the singer plead for us to "sing with one voice"?

• Can you think of a time when you and a friend "agreed to disagree"? What can the church learn from this?

Read Colossians 4:7-18, then discuss these questions in your group:
• What do these verses say about teamwork?

• Do you think all the people mentioned in this passage needed each other? Why or why not?

• How did the people mentioned in this passage support each other?

• Do you think you need to be supported in that way, too? Why or why not?

• What other ways could your Christian friends support and encourage you to follow Jesus every day?

• How can you support and encourage others to make Jesus the point of their lives?

A Focused Life

"See to it that you complete the work you have received in the Lord."
—Colossians 4:17

"SEE TO IT THAT YOU COMPLETE THE WORK YOU HAVE RECEIVED IN THE LORD." —COLOSSIANS 4:17

"See to it that you complete the work you have received in the Lord."
—Colossians 4:17

"See to it that you complete the work you have received in the Lord." —Colossians 4:17

GET TO THE POINT!

Share It

By the end of this week, your challenge is to accomplish each of the following tasks: (As you achieve each goal, put a check mark beside it.)

1. Tell at least three different people one or more godly qualities you admire in each of them.

2. Tell at least five people what you believe is the point of life.

3. Ask at least two of your Christian friends how you can better support and encourage them in their faith, then do whatever they request.

4. Pray for at least five of your Christian friends—that they would focus their lives on following Jesus every day.

5. Ask at least two Christian friends to pray for you—that you would focus your life on following Jesus every day.

6. List at least three other ways you can help yourself to stay focused on Jesus this week. Then choose one of them and do it.

7. At the end of the week, tell at least one person how accomplishing #1-6 has impacted your life.

What's Our Point?

After you've finished the six sessions in this book, give your teenagers a chance to put what they've learned into action through this creative project. Based on their study of Colossians, your students will work together to come up with an answer to the question, "What's our point as a group?" Is it to share the gospel? Serve the elderly? Reach out to the needy? Teach younger kids? Some combination of all of these? Your teens will decide.

Then, based on the point your group creates, your students will design and execute a special project that demonstrates their point to others. For example, they might design an outreach to a nursing home, take over a children's Sunday school class for a week, form "prayer teams" to pray weekly on their school campus or some combination of these ideas. Anything is possible!

Focus

This is a special event—a planned special project that students create and execute based on their desire to follow Jesus and make a point together as a group.

Before Point Day

Near the end of your six-week study, invite your teenagers to a special meeting. At the start of the meeting, say, **"Through our study of Colossians, we've learned that the real point of life is to love and follow Jesus with all of our hearts and minds. We've also explored many ways each of us can individually demonstrate the point of our lives with family members, co-workers and friends. Now it's time to consider a larger question: What should our point be as a group? We know we should love and follow Jesus, but what does that look like in a group setting like this one? What's the message our group wants to project about the point of life? How should we work together to demonstrate what we believe?"**

Form groups of five or fewer and give each group paper and writing utensils. Have groups work together to come up with a statement that defines what they think your youth group's point should be. Tell groups to write their statements this way: "The point of our group should be to love and follow Jesus by. . . ." Encourage groups to complete the statement with specific ideas on how they think the group should demonstrate devotion to Christ.

As the groups work, tape a sheet of newsprint to the wall. When they finish, ask a volunteer from each group to share what his or her group came up with. Write each group's statement on the newsprint. Then invite the whole group to work together to create one unified statement based on all the groups' answers. It's OK if the statement is long and lists several different "expressions" of your group's point. That will give students greater options for project ideas and help everyone take ownership of the statement.

Once the statement is complete, say, **"Now that we know what our point is, let's brainstorm some more specific ways we can take action to live out this point in the real world."**

Have students return to their original groups to work together to brainstorm creative projects they could do that would demonstrate the group's point in concrete ways. Use the suggestions on page 59 to help spark ideas, but let students ultimately decide what they want to do.

Once all the groups have a few ideas, bring all the groups together and repeat the decision-making process you used before. Write all the ideas on newsprint, then have them vote on or amend the ideas until the whole group agrees on a particular project. (If your group can't seem to choose between two or three projects, don't worry about it. Just pick one to do now, and do the rest later in the year.)

Once your group decides on a plan of action, form new teams and assign each team different responsibilities to help accomplish the project. For example, you might need some teams to collect supplies, create crafts or perhaps make phone calls. Make sure every person is directly involved in some way.

Once the responsibilities are assigned, work with your students to set a date for the project. Create a detailed schedule for the day's events—including:

- where and what time you will meet to start the day
- who will make sure all the necessary supplies are ready to go
- who will transport the group to the project site(s) (if needed)
- how each person will be involved in the task
- where everyone will meet after the project to celebrate their success

Point Day

When the big day arrives, invite your group to arrive early for a time of prayer. Read through Colossians 3:5—4:6 again and encourage students to focus on Jesus as the point of the event they're about to undertake. Also use this time to take care of any last-minute details.

After the project, gather at a designated location for a celebration. At some point during the celebration, lead students to discuss the following questions:

- **How does it feel to accomplish what you did today?**
- **Do you think we made our group's point clear to others? to ourselves?**
- **Through this project, how have you followed the teachings we've studied in Colossians over the past several weeks?**
- **How do you hope people will be impacted by our group today?**
- **How were you impacted today?**
- **Do you think you've changed because of this study? Why or why not?**
- **Do you think your life will be different as a result of the study and today's experience? Why or why not?**
- **Based on today's experience, what one change do you really want to see happen in your life?**

- **What do you need from this group to help you apply what we've learned in this study to your life from now on?**

After the discussion, have students share how they've seen other group members grow or change as a result of this study and today's experience. Once again, congratulate them on their efforts and encourage them to let this experience become the launching point for other adventures the group can do to demonstrate their point to others and encourage people to focus on following Jesus.

IDEA-STARTERS FOR POINT-DAY PROJECTS

Here are some options your teens might consider as creative ways to demonstrate the group's point to others:

- Bake cookies and take them to a nursing home or retirement center in your community. After delivering the cookies, have students spend time visiting with the residents.
- Offer to mow the yards of the homes around your church for free; or, if your church isn't near any homes, choose a residential neighborhood somewhere close by. After mowing the yards, leave an invitation on the doorstep for residents to come visit your church. (Make sure students do a good job mowing, raking and sweeping the sidewalk.)
- Start a morning Bible study and prayer group on the school campus. Pray every week for fellow students and teachers, asking God to bring revival to the school.
- Go on a one-day mission trip with an inner-city ministry. Repair damaged homes, work with children, or share the gospel in the streets.
- Design a fundraiser for a cause your teens believe in and want to support.
- Volunteer as a group to serve local social service agencies. For example, students could provide meals for the homeless or play with foster children.
- Create an outreach event for non-Christian friends. During the event, invite teens from your group to share their testimonies and invite others to become Christians.
- Visit the hospital and pray for the sick.
- Have a 24-hour prayer vigil and pray for your church's leadership, revival in our country, your youth group, unsaved friends and family members. As a follow-up, establish a prayer chain so that any group member with a need can easily contact the whole group to ask for prayer support.
- For a week or more, have your teens take over a children's Sunday school class.
- Create "care packages" or gifts to send to college students in your church. Pray together often for them and regularly send them encouraging notes to let them know your group is supporting them and praying for them.

notes

INTRODUCTION

[1]Adapted from *Extraordinary Results From Ordinary Teachers*, by Michael D. Warden (Group, 1998), p. 157. Used by permission.

Other EMPOWERED™ YOUTH PRODUCTS from Standard Publishing